A Note from the Composer

I looked forward to returning to the imaginative world created by J.R.R. Tolkien for quite some time. I read all of Tolkien's books, including *The Hobbit*, when I was in my 20s. My inspiration begins with the book. Tolkien's love of nature and all things green is one that resonates deeply with me.

The Hobbit revisits several of Tolkien's cultures—Hobbits, Dwarves, Elves, and Wizards. The main focus is the Dwarves' quest for Erebor and the home they left behind, now closely guarded by the Dragon, Smaug. As I worked on the film, I always had the book on my desk as a guide, reading it as I composed and then again when I was orchestrating. My connection with Tolkien's work inspires me to express that connection in music.

I find that choosing the musical palette for a film is a lot like casting—it is important to match the sound of the music to the essence of the story. The London Philharmonic Orchestra has a unique and beautiful sound that is well suited to bringing the world of Middle-earth to life.

My hope is that with this folio you too can express your own interpretation of Middle-earth.

Happy music making!

—Howard Shore

THE HOBBIT
AN UNEXPECTED JOURNEY

Music Composed by HOWARD SHORE
Sheet Music Selections from the Original Motion Picture Soundtrack

CONTENTS

Produced by
Alfred Music Publishing Co., Inc.
P.O. Box 10003
Van Nuys, CA 91410-0003
alfred.com

Printed in USA.

ISBN-10: 0-7390-9159-X
ISBN-13: 978-0-7390-9159-3

MY DEAR FRODO

Lyrics by
PHILIPPA BOYENS

Music by
HOWARD SHORE

Moderately (♩ = 118)

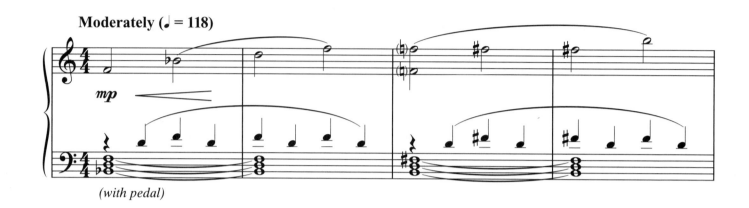

(with pedal)

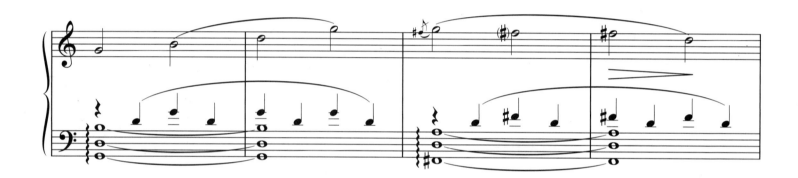

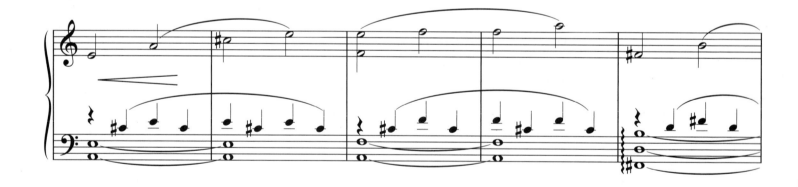

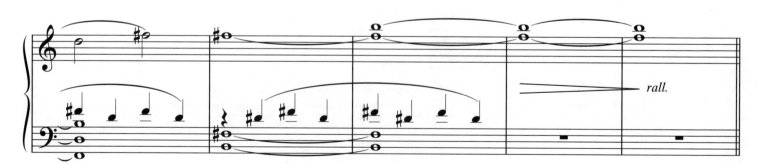

My Dear Frodo - 14 - 1

Slower (♩ = 84)

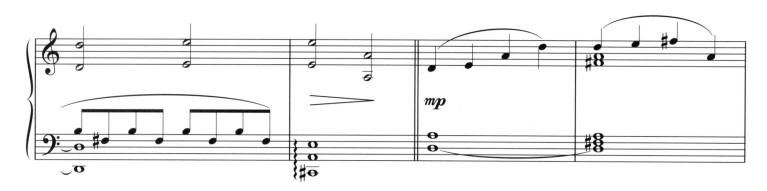

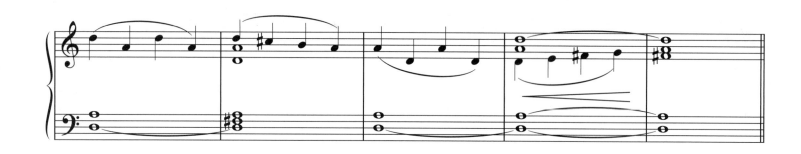

Nin hweh see lee mee seh nar noh ah seel_____ mah nah.

Men:

Ni gah nahd_____ ah noo ni gah nad_____

ah nool._____ Du kim an_____ nan rah._____

Kah ahr sah_____ lu dah._____

a little faster (♩ = 104)

Brightly (♩ = 92)

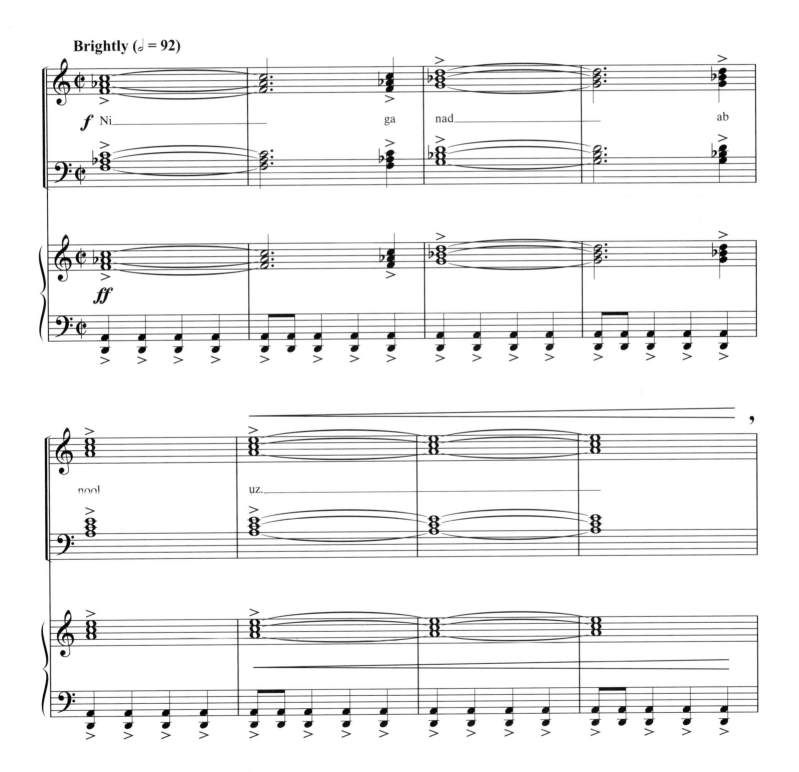

Ni_____ ga nad_____ ab

nool_____ uz._____

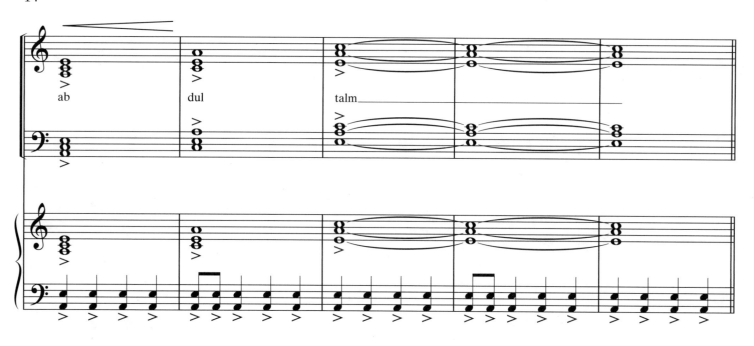

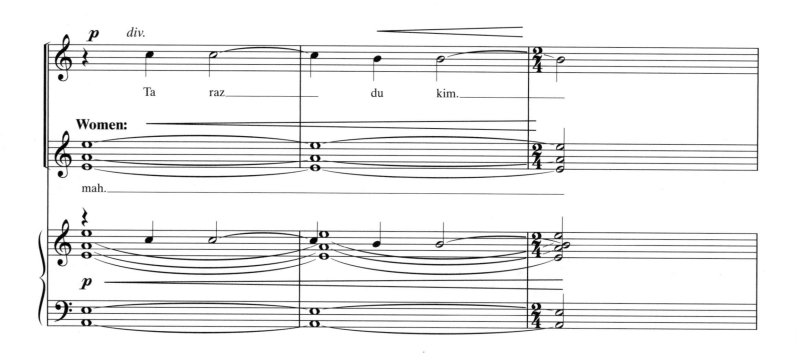

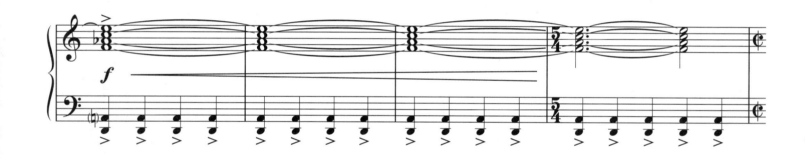

OLD FRIENDS

Music by
HOWARD SHORE

Slowly (♩ = 81)

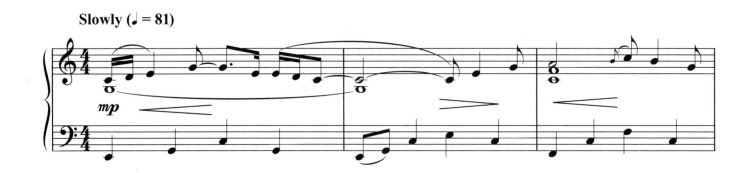

Old Friends - 6 - 1

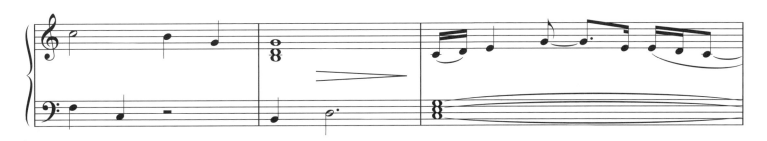

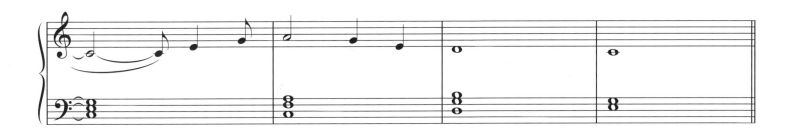

A little faster (♩ =104)

Old Friends - 6 - 2

Slower (♩ = 82)

Slower (♩ = 56)

Moderately (♩=104)

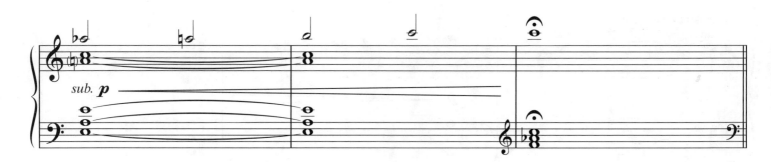

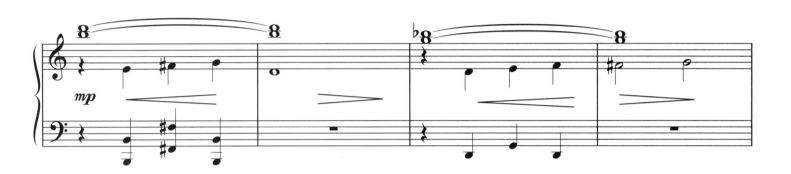

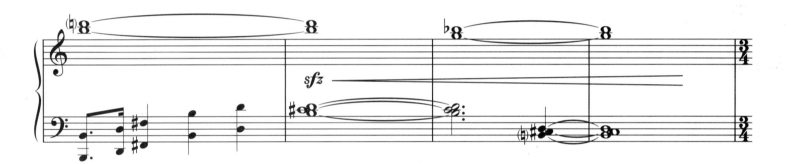

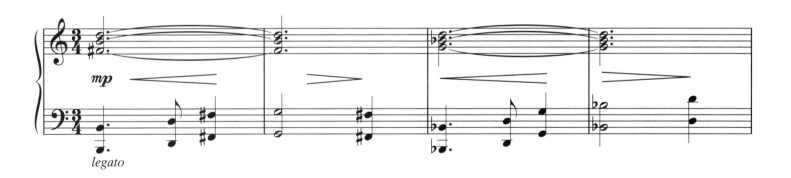

AN UNEXPECTED PARTY

Music by
HOWARD SHORE

Moderately (♩ = 104)

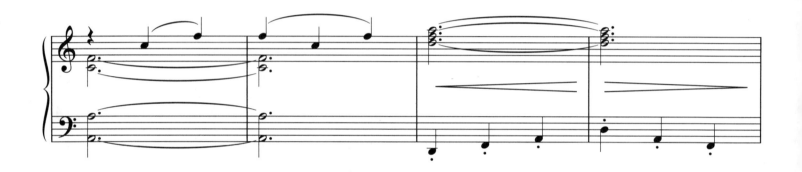

An Unexpected Party - 6 - 1

a little faster (♩= 116)

Moderately bright (♩ = 131)

a little slower (♩ = 116)

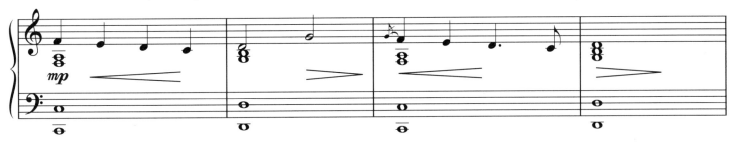

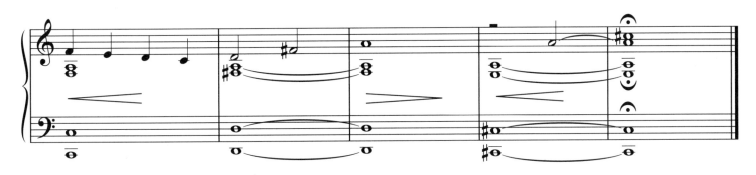

AXE OR SWORD?

Music by
HOWARD SHORE

Moderately (♩=116)

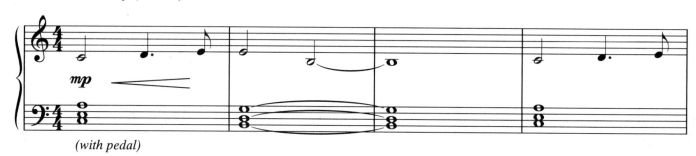

(with pedal)

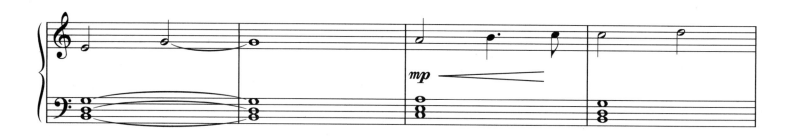

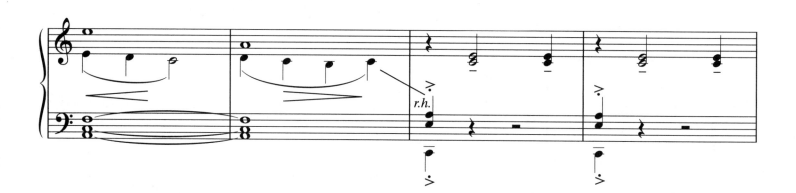

Axe or Sword? - 7 - 1

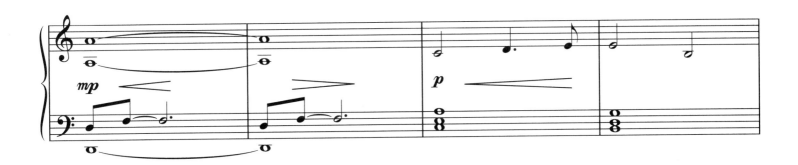

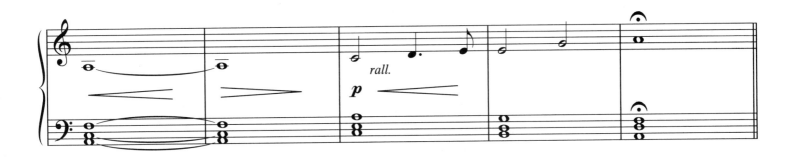

Moderately ($\quarternote$ = 96)

Moderately (♩ = 96)

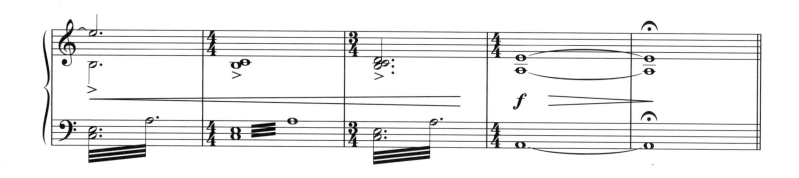

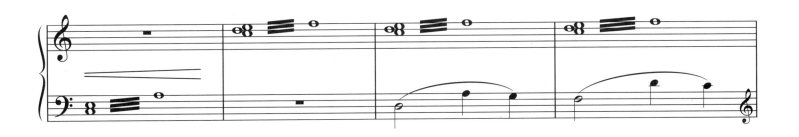

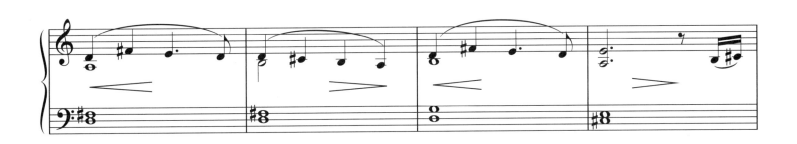

Axe or Sword? - 7 - 6

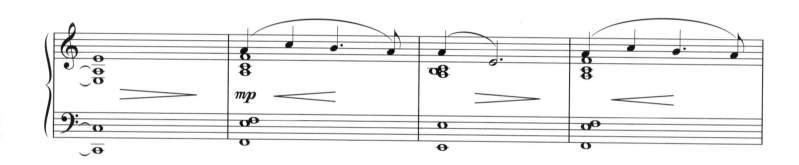

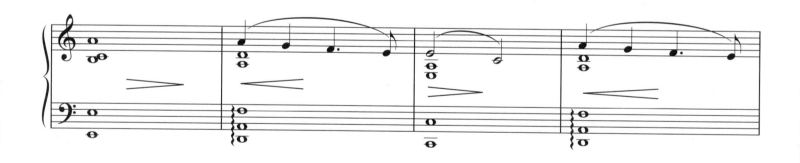

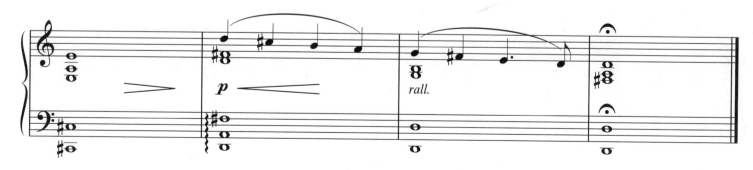

MISTY MOUNTAINS

Lyrics by
J.R.R. TOLKIEN

Music by
DAVID DONALDSON, DAVID LONG,
STEVE ROCHE and JANET RODDICK

Moderate chant, sung freely (♩ = 104)

Austerely

Far o-

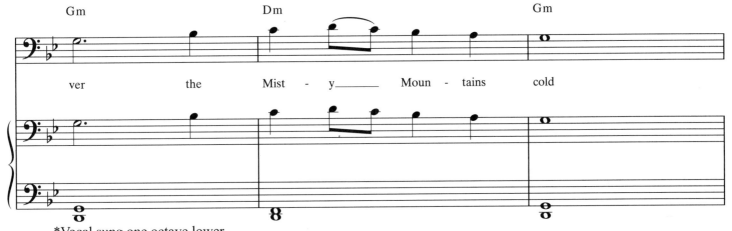

ver   the   Mist - y___ Moun - tains   cold

*Vocal sung one octave lower.

Misty Mountains - 3 - 1

THE ADVENTURE BEGINS

Music by
HOWARD SHORE

Moderately bright (♩ = 156)

The Adventure Begins - 2 - 1

RADAGAST THE BROWN

Lyrics by
PHILIPPA BOYENS

Music by
HOWARD SHORE

Moderately (♩ = 116)

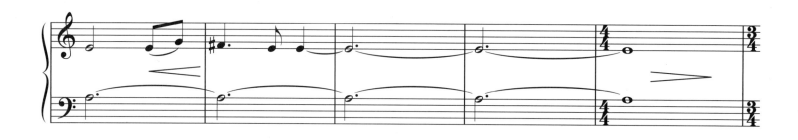

Boys Choir:

Men aw ed ven aw gah lahd vawss,

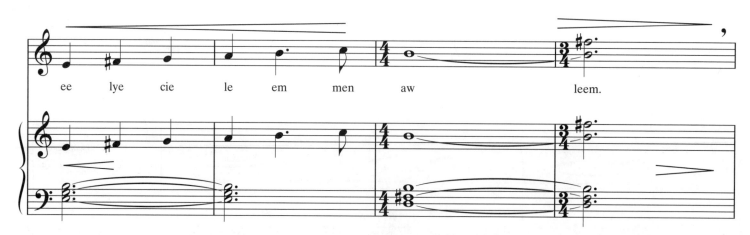

ee lye cie le em men aw leem.

Radagast the Brown - 8 - 1

Moderately slow (♩ = 72)

Leem   men   aw   leem   na   foo   een   tree.

46

48

Boys Choir:

Men awr ed ven aw gah lah - vass ee lee lem men

aw lee na - foo, hee tree doo ith ah ga ee - thraw

neg ah boy ah fah dah tham aw vee geh._____

WARG-SCOUTS

Music by
HOWARD SHORE

Agitated (♩ = 180)

Warg-Scouts - 7 - 1

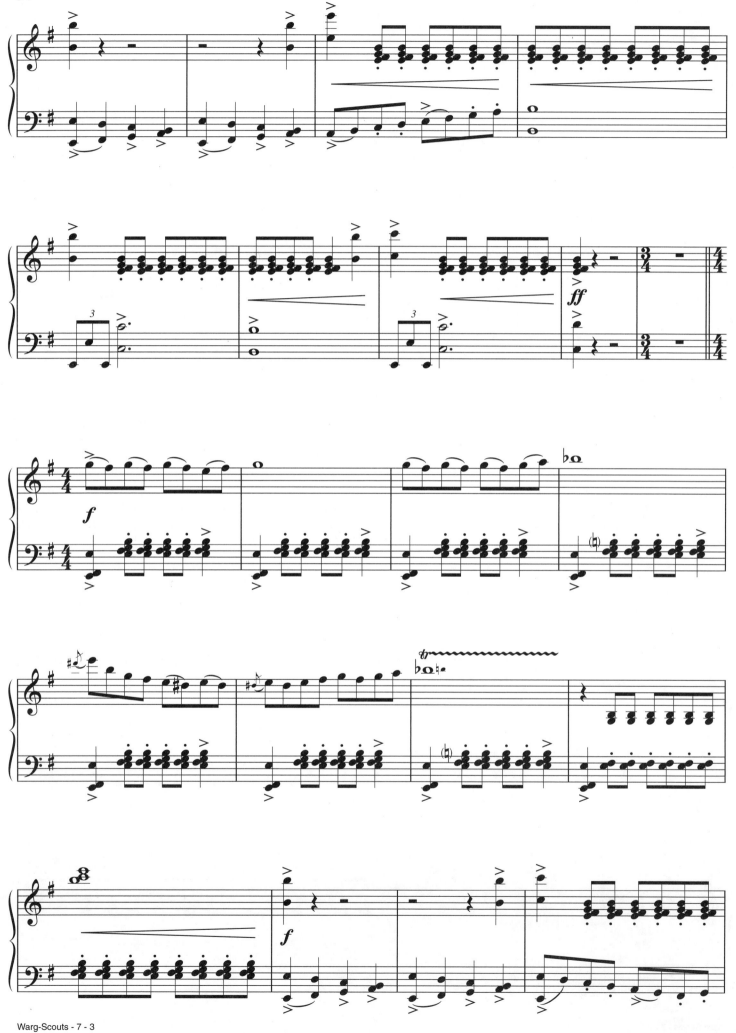

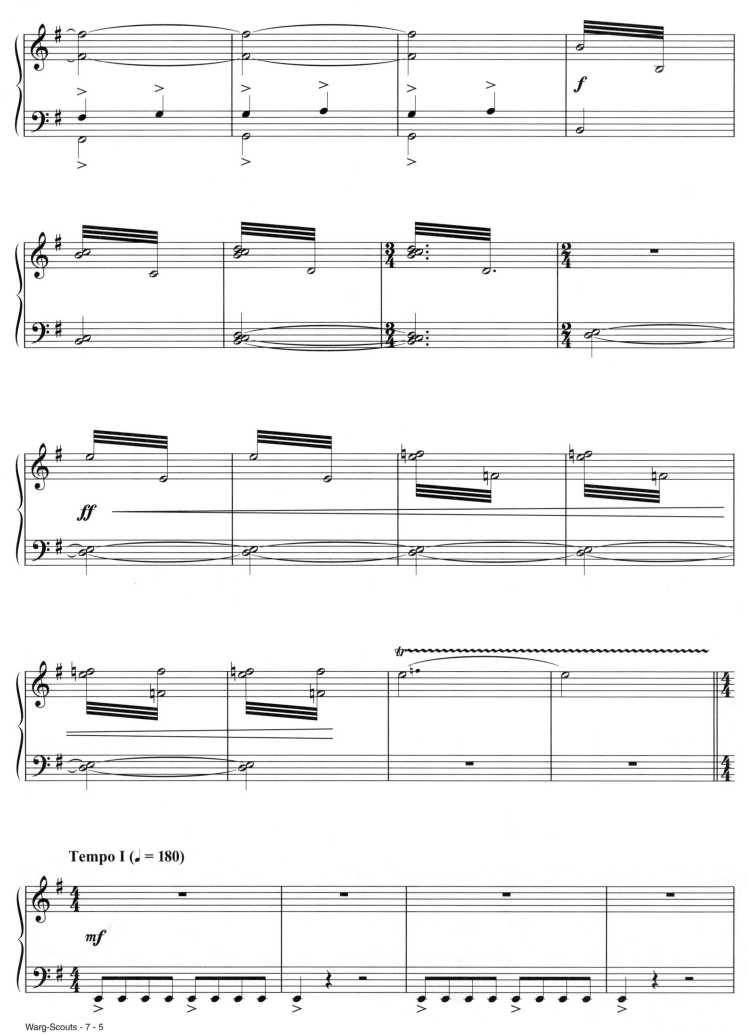

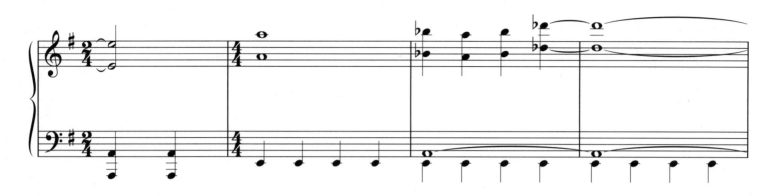

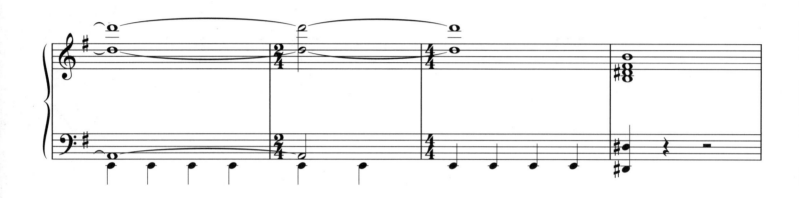

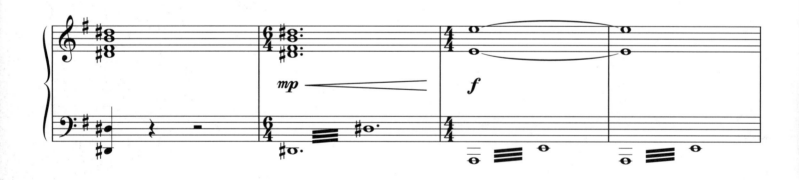

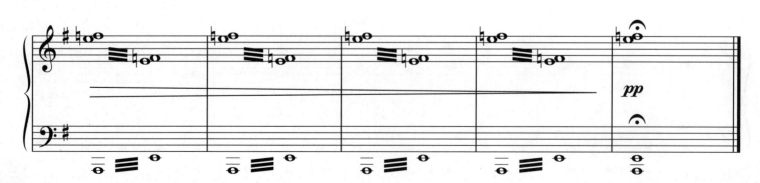

A GOOD OMEN

Lyrics by
J.R.R. TOLKIEN
Adapted by
PHILIPPA BOYENS

Music by
HOWARD SHORE

With spirit (♩ = 126)
Women:

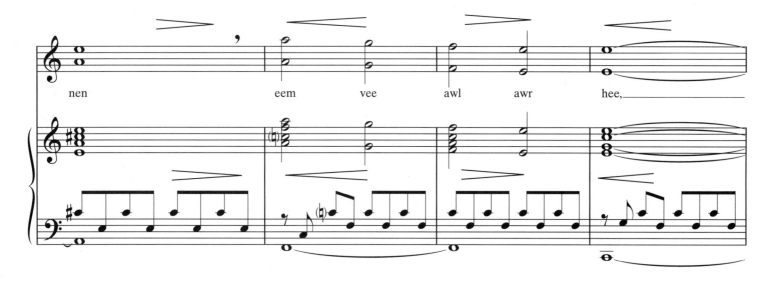

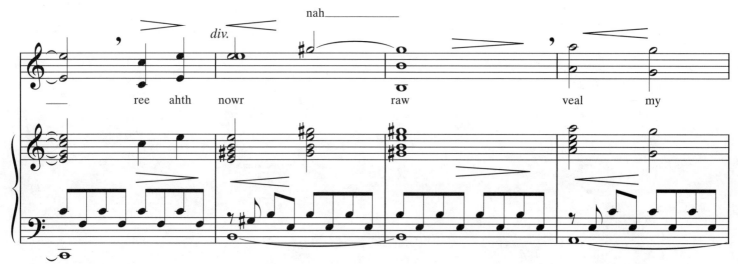

A Good Omen - 8 - 1

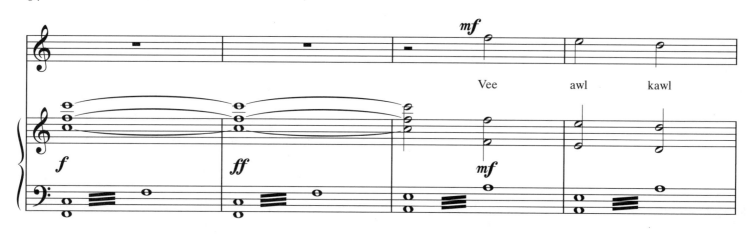

Vee   awl   kawl

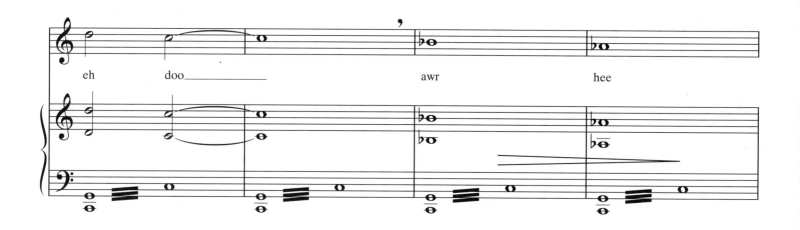

eh   doo_____   awr   hee

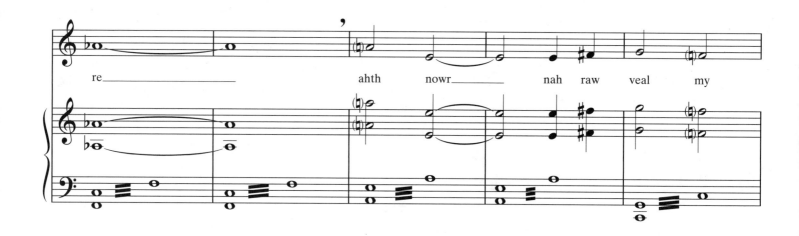

re_____   ahth   nowr_____   nah   raw   veal   my

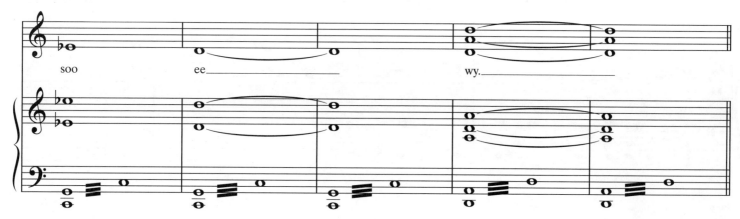

soo   ee_____   wy._____

Moderately slow (♩ = 72)

Choir:

Oo   mahn   press.

SONG OF THE LONELY MOUNTAIN

Lyrics by
NEIL FINN

Music Composed by
NEIL FINN, DAVID DONALDSON,
DAVID LONG, STEVE ROCHE
and JANET RODDICK

Song of the Lonely Mountain - 9 - 1

All_ eyes on the hid-den door, to the Lone - ly Moun-tain borne.

We'll ride in the gath-er-ing storm un - til we get our long - for-got - ten

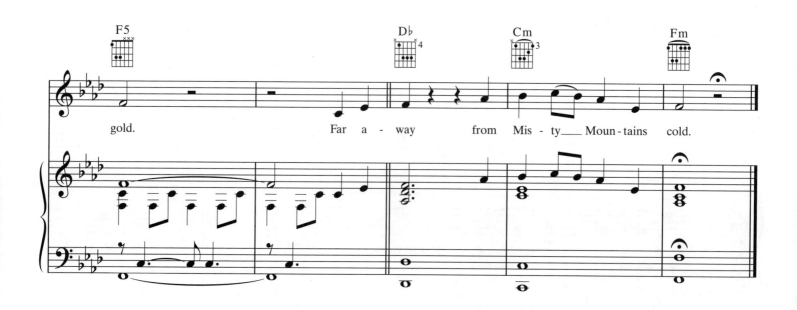

gold. Far a - way from Mis - ty_ Moun-tains cold.

DREAMING OF BAG END

Music by
HOWARD SHORE

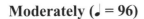

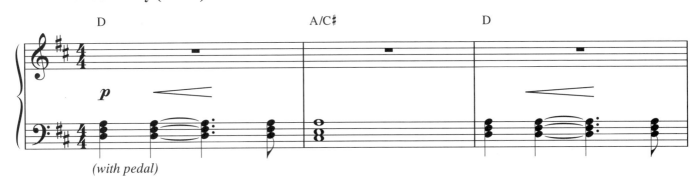

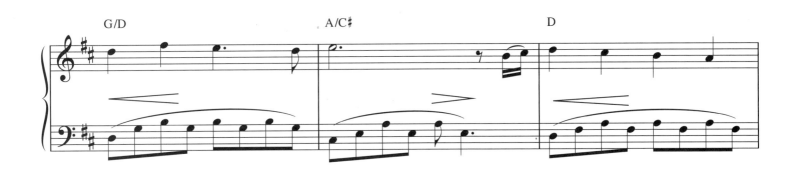

Dreaming of Bag End - 3 - 1

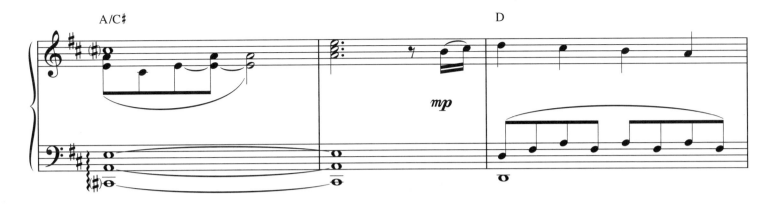

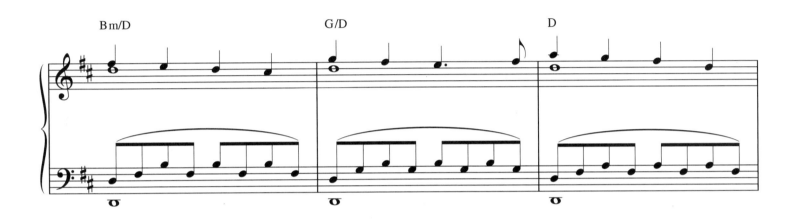

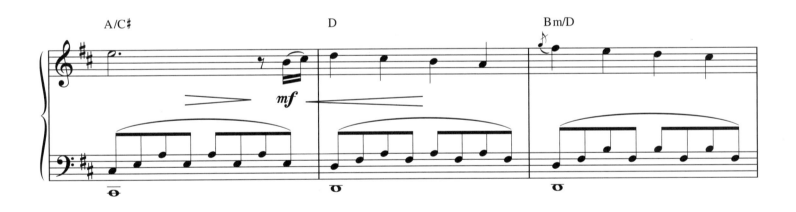

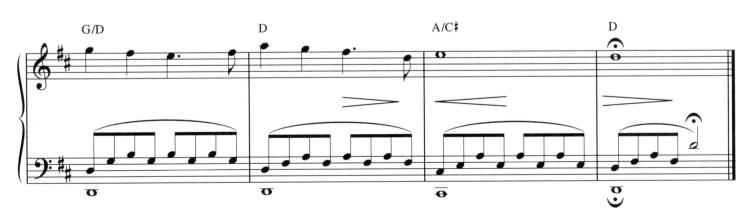

Dreaming of Bag End - 3 - 3

A VERY RESPECTABLE HOBBIT

Music by
HOWARD SHORE

A Very Respectable Hobbit - 2 - 1

EREBOR

Music by
HOWARD SHORE

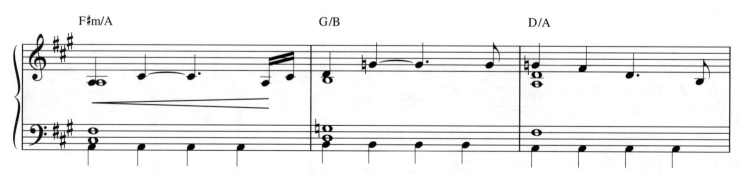

Erebor - 3 - 1

THE DWARF LORDS

Music by
HOWARD SHORE

Moderately (♩ = 104)

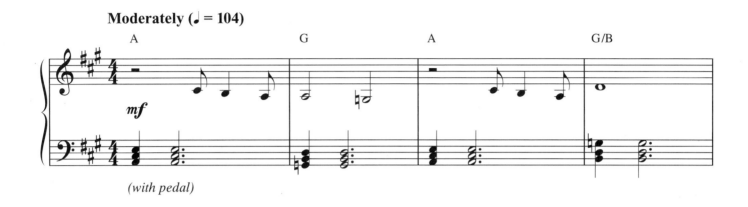

(with pedal)

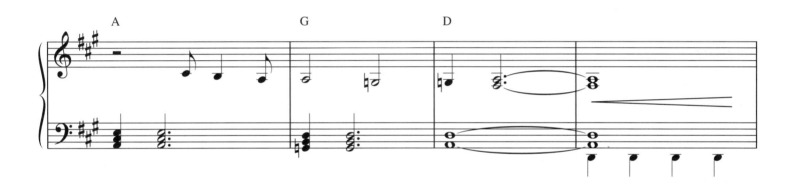

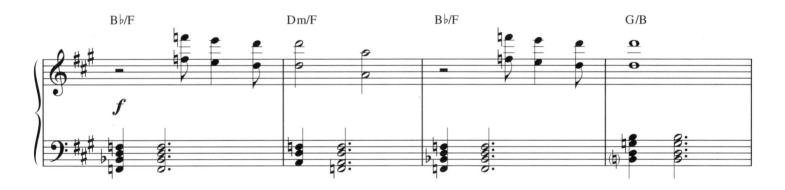

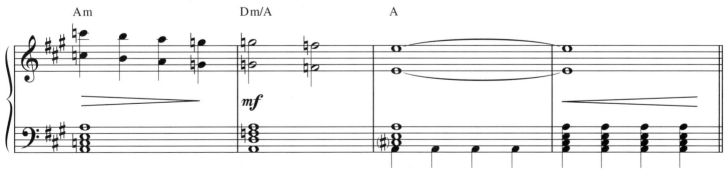

The Dwarf Lords - 3 - 1

A little slower (♩ = 92)

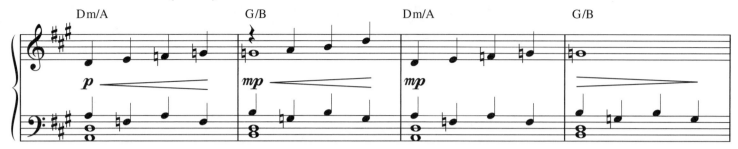

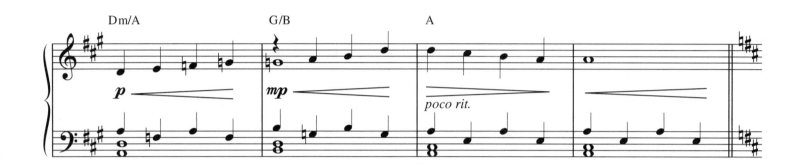

Tempo I (♩ = 104)

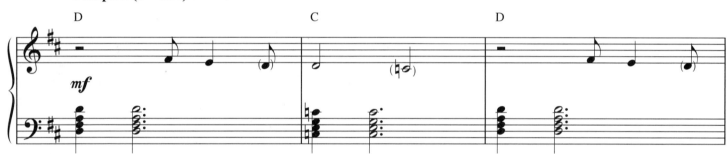

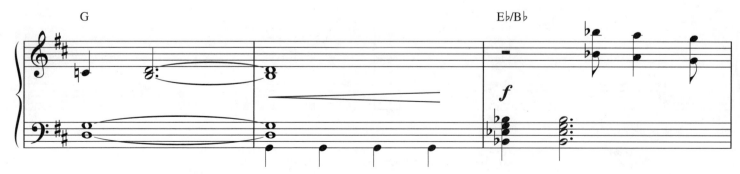

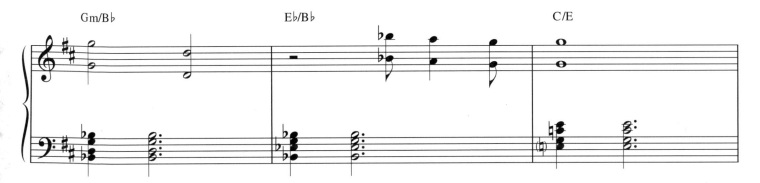

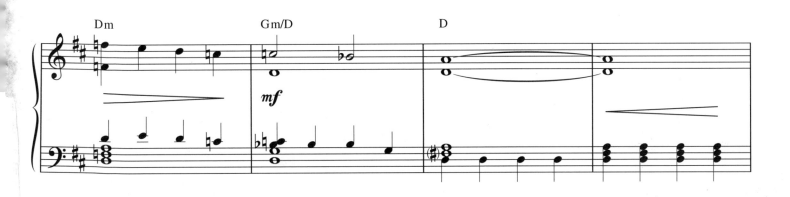

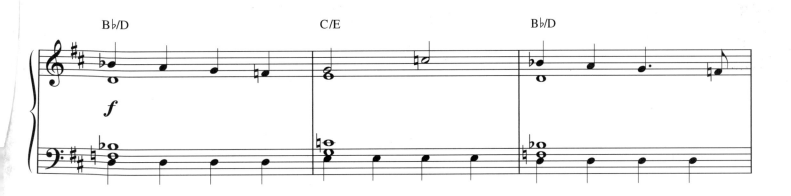

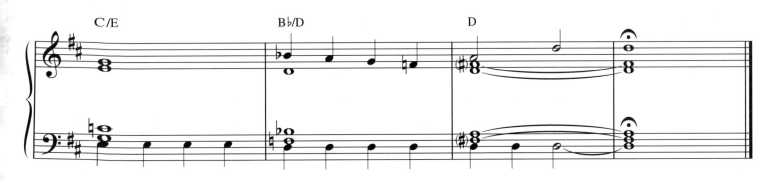